# A is for Astoria

Written by Karen L. Leedom
Illustrated by Sally Bailey

Rivertide Publishing
Astoria, OR  USA
www.rivertidepublishing.com

A is for Astoria
by Karen L. Leedom

ISBN: 978-0-9826252-0-0

Printed in Korea

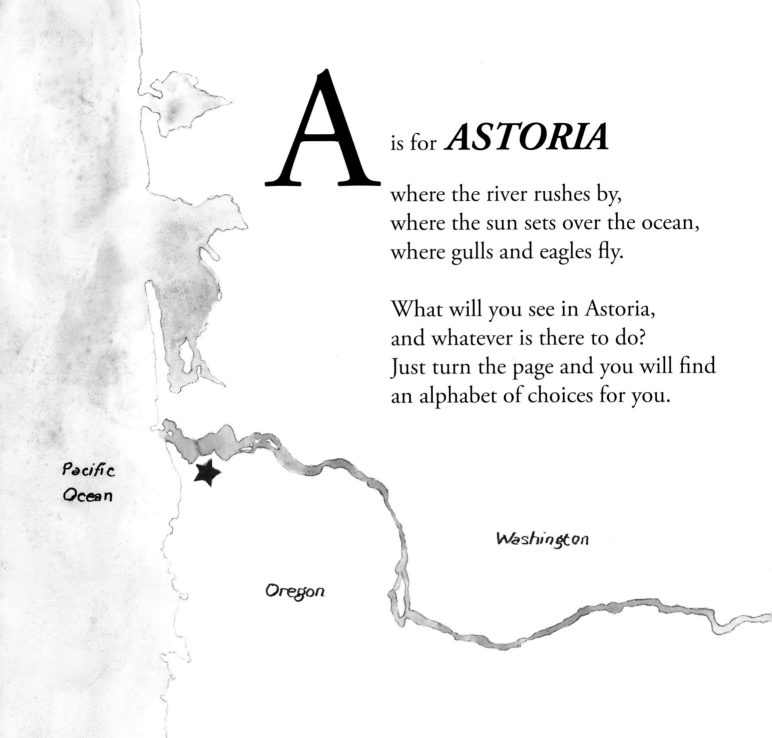

# A is for ***ASTORIA***

where the river rushes by,
where the sun sets over the ocean,
where gulls and eagles fly.

What will you see in Astoria,
and whatever is there to do?
Just turn the page and you will find
an alphabet of choices for you.

Pacific
Ocean

Washington

Oregon

*for Abby and Danny*
*and*
*for Morgain*

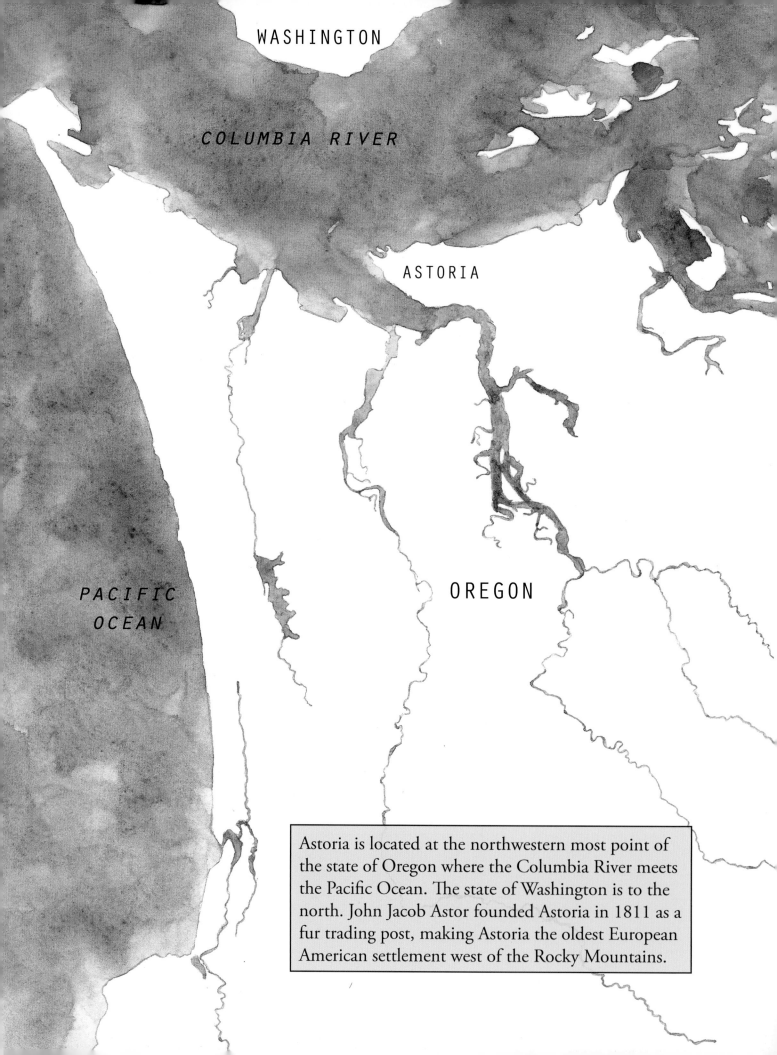

WASHINGTON

COLUMBIA RIVER

ASTORIA

PACIFIC
OCEAN

OREGON

Astoria is located at the northwestern most point of the state of Oregon where the Columbia River meets the Pacific Ocean. The state of Washington is to the north. John Jacob Astor founded Astoria in 1811 as a fur trading post, making Astoria the oldest European American settlement west of the Rocky Mountains.

# A is for the *ASTORIA COLUMN*

standing tall and straight.
It sits on top of Coxcomb Hill
with pictures quite ornate.
The images tell stories
of those early pioneers,
who made their way to Astoria
from across the vast frontier.

Completed in 1926, the Astoria
Column is 125 feet tall with 164
spiral steps leading to a viewing
platform. Painted illustrations
pay tribute to Astoria's history,
from Captain Robert Gray's
discovery of the Columbia River
to the arrival of the railroad.

# B is for the *BRIDGE*

that spans the river north and south.
Between the states the traffic flows across Columbia's mouth.
Before the bridge, a ferry was the way to make the trip.
In ancient times, a strong canoe, or perhaps a sailing ship.

The Astoria Bridge spans a distance of four miles across the river between the states of Oregon and Washington. Completed in 1966, it is the longest continuous truss bridge in the world, with a main arch 1,232 feet long. The bridge was built to withstand wind gusts of 150 miles per hour.

The Columbia River is the largest river flowing into the Pacific Ocean along the coasts of North and South America. Beginning its 1,200 mile journey in British Columbia, Canada, this mighty river emerges from Columbia Lake, between the Rocky Mountains to the east and Purcell Mountains to the west. It initially flows northwestward before turning south through Washington, where it is joined by the Snake River. The Columbia then turns westward, forming the border between Oregon and Washington.

# C is for **CLAMMING**

with your family on the beach.
Those slippery ones tunneling down just slightly out of reach.
Rise early on a foggy morn' with shovel and boots in tow.
Dig swiftly now, you must be quick, or empty-handed you'll go.

Digging for razor clams is a popular activity along the beaches of Oregon and southwest Washington. These clams can quickly burrow into the sand, so the clam digger must move fast to retrieve them.

Dungeness crabs are crustaceans, having an exterior skeleton or shell. They inhabit the Pacific Ocean from the Aleutian Islands in Alaska to south of San Francisco, California. Typically they are less than eight inches in size. When harvesting, only male crabs of a certain size may be taken.

# D is for the ***DUNGENESS CRABS***

that live in the northwest sea.
With hardened shells and pincers sharp,
they sidle from you and from me.
Into the water you lower your pot,
hoping to fill your sack.
Do not be hasty, measure you must,
for the small ones must always go back.

# E is for the *ELK*

along the roadways as you pass.
They amble through the foothills in search of tender grass.
Gathering in nearby fields in groups of ten or more,
these beasts are large and powerful, not easy to ignore.

Roosevelt elk are the largest of the big game animals. A mature bull may weigh 1,000 pounds or more. They like to eat huckleberry, blackberry, and other shrubs, as well as weeds and grasses. One place to view elk in the wild is at the Jewell Elk Refuge east of Astoria on Highway 202.

# F is for the *FISHERMEN*

who take their boats to sea,
and catch the salmon, crab and shrimp,
so good, for you and me.
Sometimes the seas are raging, but the men they do abide,
until at last they fill their nets and sail home with the tide.

Over one-hundred years ago Astoria was known as the salmon capital of the world, so fishing has always been important to the local economy. Gillnet fishing began in the 1850s and continues today. Netting is laid across a stretch of water and the salmon's gills become entangled in the webbing.

Several gull species are found along the Northwest Coast. Most gulls will eat anything they can catch or scavenge. When they spot someone with food, gulls swoop in to take advantage.

# G is for the **GULLS**

who like to catch the wind and soar.
All gray and white,
they sometimes come to gather on the shore.
They often, though, will swoop in close
if you have bread to share.
Just watch them dart around your head
as you toss it in the air.

There are many hiking trails in the Pacific Northwest. In Astoria, the Richard Fencsak Cathedral Tree Trail leads from 28th & Irving Streets to the Astoria Column. The Fort to Sea Trail (pictured here), will take you from Fort Clatsop to the Pacific Ocean, following a path used by Lewis & Clark during the winter of 1805-06.

# H is for *HIKING*

in the mountains, through the trees.
Among the shrubs and bushes
you may wander as you please.
You might find it interesting to venture up a hill,
or strolling by a mountain stream
may give you quite a thrill.

DENMARK

SWEDEN

FINLAND

NORWAY

People from many countries
settled in Astoria, with a large
number arriving from Scandinavia
and Finland. In the early 1900s
there were more Finns living in
Astoria than any other nationality.

NORWEGIAN SEA

SWEDEN

FINLAND

NORWAY

DENMARK

I is for *IMMIGRANTS*

from countries far away,
who somehow found Astoria
and decided they would stay.
By boat and wagon train they came,
intent to make their mark,
from far off lands like Finland,
Sweden, Norway and Denmark.

# J is for the *JETTY*

built of boulders that are large,
brought in from distant places by truck and train and barge.
Climb upon the viewing stage on a stormy, windy day,
and watch the waves come crashing in, and feel your body sway.

The entrance from the Pacific Ocean to the Columbia River has always been troublesome for vessels crossing in or out. To remedy this, construction began in 1885 on a five-mile long jetty near Fort Stevens. A short railroad transported the gigantic boulders needed to construct the jetty, with some exceeding fifty tons. There is a viewing platform where you can watch the waves crash against the rocks.

K is for the **KITE**

that teeters softly on the breeze.
You hold it tight with all your might,
it dips and dives with ease.
Run and run to catch the wind, and let it freely fly.
Then watch your kite as it takes flight and rises in the sky.

Frequent ocean breezes create perfect conditions for flying kites. Many beach communities have kite flying festivals, like the International Kite Festival in Long Beach, Washington, held in August each year.

# L is for the *LIGHTHOUSE*

sitting high upon the land,
that sends a beam to ships at sea, and lends a helping hand.
Many shipwrecks did occur before this light did glow.
Vessels in the dark of night could not see where to go.

Cape Disappointment Lighthouse in the state of Washington was built in 1856 and is the oldest standing lighthouse in the Pacific Northwest. North Head, also in Washington, was completed in 1898 on one of the windiest spots on the West Coast, with gusts recorded up to 120 mph. Ships were also used to light the way into the Columbia River until 1979. The last lightship in service on the West Coast was the Columbia River No. 604, currently on display at the Columbia River Maritime Museum.

NORTH HEAD

CAPE DISAPPOINTMENT

LIGHTSHIP

COLUMBIA

# M is for *MUSEUMS*

that are filled with ancient things,
like maps and charts and journals,
and necklaces and rings.
Books and clothes and trinkets
on the shelves and on the wall,
you never know what treasures
may be found just down the hall.

FLAVEL
HOUSE
MUSEUM

Astoria has unique and
interesting museums,
like the elegant home
built in 1885 by Captain
George Flavel, Columbia
River bar pilot and the
area's first millionaire.
The Heritage Museum
is home to the historical
society's archive and
local history museum.
Founded in 1962,
the Columbia River
Maritime Museum is the
official maritime museum
of the state of Oregon.

HERITAGE MUSEUM

COLUMBIA RIVER MARITIME MUSEUM

# N is for *NATIVE AMERICANS*

the Clatsop and Chinook,
who lived here first, for thousands of years,
as told in the history books.
A friendly welcome they did give
to Lewis & Clark long ago,
but when the settlers came along,
the Indians were forced to go.

The Clatsop and Chinook tribes lived along the Northern Oregon and Southwest Washington coasts for thousands of years before settlers came to the area. They traded with early explorers and welcomed Lewis & Clark. But as more and more people arrived from the eastern United States, these early Americans were forced to move from their native lands.

# O is for the **OCEAN**

that rushes in and out.
Sometimes it is so noisy
that you feel you need to shout.
Tumbling waves come roaring in,
they curl around your feet.
The vast Pacific Ocean
is the largest one you'll meet.

Our planet is approximately seventy-one percent water and has five oceans: the Arctic, Atlantic, Indian, Pacific and Southern (or Antarctic). The Pacific Ocean is the largest of these oceans.

Federal law requires all ships entering the
Columbia River to carry a licensed bar pilot. The
bar pilot navigates the vessel to Astoria. If the
ship is continuing to an upriver port, piloting
is transferred to a river pilot who navigates the
vessel to its final destination. When a ship heads
out to sea, this process is reversed.

P is for the **PILOTS**

who steer and lead the way,
across the bar and up the river,
they do this every day.
They climb aboard a moving ship
that does not stop or slow.
They take the helm and gain control,
knowing precisely where to go.

# Q is for the *QUARANTINE STATION*

built to combat disease,
where ships from far off lands were checked
before they could do as they please.
Sailing ships would have to stop
and dock at Knappton's pier,
where passengers were sanitized,
along with all their gear.

To fight diseases like bubonic plague and small pox, Congress in 1891 passed a law requiring the medical inspection of all arriving immigrants. In 1899, the Columbia River Quarantine Station opened on the north shore of the river. All ships were inspected, and if fumigation or quarantine were warranted, they anchored at Knappton Cove. Fumigation consisted of sealing the ship and boiling cauldrons of sulfur. The fumes killed rats and fleas that cause disease.

KNAPPTON COVE HERITAGE CENTER

US QUARANTINE STATION 1938

US PUBLIC HEALTH SERVICE 1938

# R is for the *RESCUES*

taking place most every day.
When someone is in trouble, help is on the way.
The Coast Guard moves in quickly
from the sea or from the air.
No matter what the weather, they bravely will be there.

The U. S. Coast Guard utilizes
motor lifeboats, helicopters,
cutters and specially trained rescue
swimmers when responding to
search and rescue incidents at sea.

# S is for the *SEA LIONS*

who lay upon the rocks.
They also have a fondness for sunning on the docks.
From up the hill you hear their sound, a loud resounding bark,
in the morning, all the day, and even after dark.

Steller and California sea lions frequent the lower Columbia River. At times, hundreds of sea lions can be found on jetties, piers and fishing docks in the river estuary. A large number often lounge on the docks at Astoria's East Mooring Basin, where their loud barking can be heard all over town. Sea lions eat a variety of marine prey, and are especially fond of salmon.

# T is for the *TROLLEY*

Step aboard and find a seat.
A trip along the river will give you such a treat.
Back and forth along the track it rings a big brass bell.
Conductors, they relate the past, and do it very well.

# U is for *UMBRELLAS*

blue, yellow, green and red,
protecting you from stormy skies,
keeping raindrops from your head.
Be careful, though, when winds do fly
and rain is streaming down.
Umbrellas can turn inside out
and leave you with a frown.

Some areas of the Pacific
Northwest receive as
much as 200 inches
of rainfall each year.
Astoria averages 70
inches of rain annually.

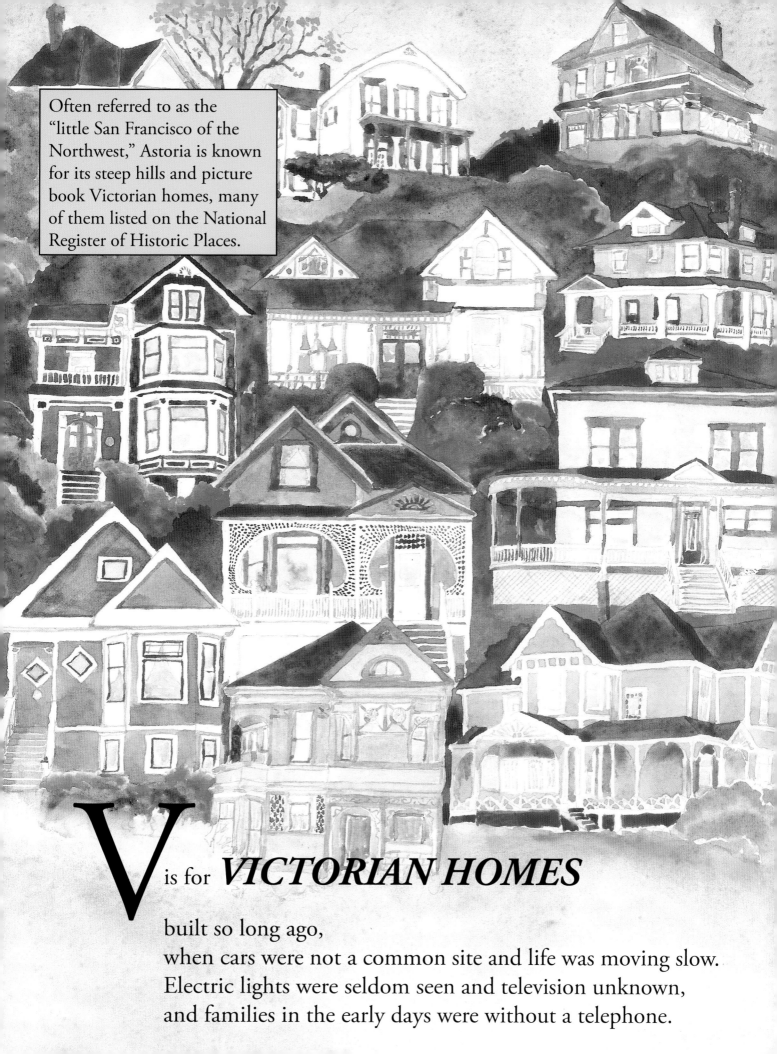

Often referred to as the "little San Francisco of the Northwest," Astoria is known for its steep hills and picture book Victorian homes, many of them listed on the National Register of Historic Places.

# V is for *VICTORIAN HOMES*

built so long ago,
when cars were not a common site and life was moving slow.
Electric lights were seldom seen and television unknown,
and families in the early days were without a telephone.

# W is for the *WAVES*

that tumble from the ocean.
Some of them are very small,
and others cause commotion.
Please beware when taking in
that salty ocean breeze.
Waves can sneak in without sound
and knock you to your knees.

Wind blowing across the ocean's surface causes waves; the stronger the wind, the larger the waves. Large waves can appear without warning, surging high onto the beaches with deadly force. These "sneaker waves" are impossible to predict, sometimes catching beachcombers off guard.

Clatsop Indian lore speaks of a Spanish ship that anchored offshore of Neahkahnie Mountain several hundred years ago. Legend says a landing party buried a treasure chest on the slopes of the mountain, marking the spot with an inscribed rock. To this day the search continues for the lost treasure of Neahkahnie Mountain.

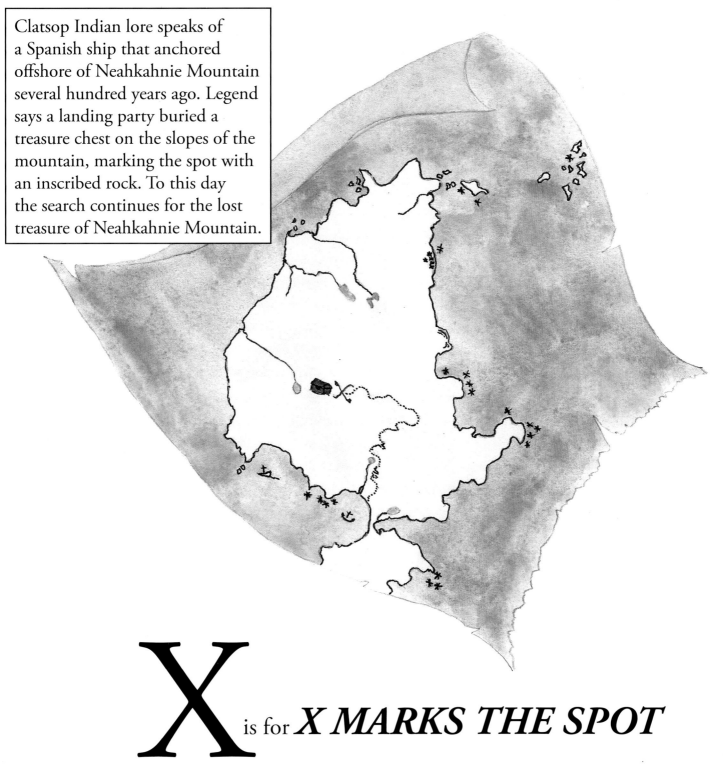

# X is for *X MARKS THE SPOT*

where buried treasure lies,
where sailors tried their best to hide
their spoils from their spies.
For centuries some folks have tried
to find that special place.
But not a one has found it yet;
it's lost without a trace.

Astoria's two mooring basins are filled with boats of all shapes and sizes, some of them expensive yachts from other parts of the world.

# Y is for the *YACHTS*

that sail, so big and bold and dear.
Around the world they travel in luxury all year.
They sometimes find Astoria and stay a day or two,
then off again to sea they go in search of someplace new.

# Z is for the *ZILLION GRAINS OF SAND*

upon the shore.
If you put them in your pail, the sea will just bring more.
Sift the sand through little fingers, poke it with your toes,
scoop it up and pour it out, away on the wind it goes.

As the Columbia River winds its way from Canada to the Pacific Ocean, its rushing waters erode the mountains in its path, turning rock into sand. The river collects this sediment along the way, and when the river crashes headlong into incoming waves, it empties its cargo. The ocean gathers up much of this sand and deposits it along the beaches of Oregon and southwest Washington.

## Author and Illustrator

Photo by Schell Photography, Astoria

Karen Leedom, left, lives in Astoria with her husband, Dan. A North Coast resident since 1998, Karen is also the author of *Astoria: An Oregon History,* and *S is for Sunriver.*

Sally Bailey, right, lived in Astoria from 2005 until her death in 2011, where she was an active and valued member of the local art community.